freshwater FISHING

Written by David Holzer
Illustrations by S. Milne & M. J. Atkinson

TOP THAT!™

Copyright © 2004 Top That! Publishing plc,
Top That! Publishing, 25031 W. Avenue Stanford,
Suite #60, Valencia, CA 91355
All rights reserved
www.topthatpublishing.com

CONTENTS

▶ Page 4   Introduction

▶ Page 6   Environment

▶ Page 8   North American Waters

▶ Page 10   Atlantic Salmon

▶ Page 13   Black Bass

▶ Page 16   Bream

▶ Page 19   Bullhead

▶ Page 22   Carp

▶ Page 25   Catfish

▶ Page 28   Crappie

▶ Page 31   Lake Whitefish

▶ Page 34   Muskellunge

▶ Page 37   Northern Pike

▶ Page 40   Pacific Salmon

▶ Page 43   Steelhead

▶ Page 46   Rainbow Trout

▶ Page 49   Trout: Brook and Lake

CONTENTS

Page 52	Walleye	◄
Page 55	White Sturgeon	◄
Page 58	Yellow Perch	◄
Page 61	Particular Species	◄
Page 62	Worldwide	◄
Page 68	Tackle	◄
Page 76	Bait	◄
Page 82	Tackle Box Items	◄
Page 84	Other Equipment	◄
Page 87	Float Fishing	◄
Page 92	Ledgering	◄
Page 98	Game Fishing	◄
Page 103	Fly-fishing	◄
Page 116	Responsible Fishing	◄
Page 122	Fish Recipes	◄
Page 126	Vital Statistics	◄
Page 128	Conclusion	

Introduction

Wherever you live, there is an enormous variety of fish to look for. Today, when waters are being carefully managed, tackle is improving all the time, and records are constantly being broken, there has never been a better time to start freshwater fishing.

There are three kinds of angler. Pleasure anglers practice their hobby simply because they enjoy it. Match anglers enjoy the added buzz of competing. Specimen anglers focus on catching big fish, as well as gathering and comparing information.

Whichever kind of angler you are, or hope to be, there is no question that the sport demands great skill and patience. But it can also be very rewarding.

This aim of this guide to freshwater fishing in North America is to provide a handy source of reference for anglers of all types, at various skill levels. Some of the fish profiled are anadromous. This means that they migrate from the sea to freshwater to spawn but can be caught in saltwater.

Wherever you are fishing, we are sure this guide will spur you on to try different techniques and broaden the range of fish you catch.

So, as they say, tight lines!

Environment

In North American waters, it's possible to fish all year round although water conditions vary a lot. The environment in which fish are found also changes from species to species.

A fundamental part of getting to grips with freshwater fishing is understanding what it means to fish in different habitats, whether in lakes, rivers, streams, or other waters. Even then, water conditions change a great deal, sometimes within the course of a single day. Learning to read different conditions is vital.

Fishing at certain times of the year demands yet another set of skills. Trying out your luck in icy weather on the same stretch of river that you fished in summer is very different. Flood conditions, high winds, and fishing in darkness also demand their own individual techniques.

You also need to know where to find the fish you're after, or at least where they should be, and you can only really do this by being able to read water conditions.

If you regularly fish the same spot for the same fish, there's no substitute for just studying the water and seeing how the fish behave. You'll learn which fish favor which snags, for instance.

HABITATS

When you're going after fish you never tried for before, in a different part of the country, it's all about learning what you can about the area and talking to people who know. For instance, it's obvious that your buddy who knows all there is to know about crappie fishing in Texas is going to be no substitute for a professional Atlantic salmon guide in Labrador.

This guide aims to give you an idea of the conditions in which you should be able to find good examples of the fish most commonly sought after in North America. But it's no substitute for actually going out and studying your subject.

North American Waters

North American waters are home to a remarkable amount of very different species of freshwater fish. Some are found in a specific type of environment and particular water conditions. Others can be caught all across the continent. There are tricks and techniques for landing every one.

Some anglers become fascinated with only one kind of fish. Carp anglers the world over are the obvious example. They devote their entire fishing lives to perfecting techniques for catching this species, and are constantly adding to their store of knowledge.

When it comes to certain fish—muskie for instance—some anglers will come back to the same stretch of water again and again, determined to catch one specific fish.

Others prefer to go after different fish, at set times of the year, in running and still waters, using a whole variety of techniques and tackle. They also spend their vacations in different parts of the country, just for the fishing.

Whichever kind of angler you are, or intend to be, it's for certain that freshwater fishing will give you a lifetime of pleasure.

Silvery to yellow brown sides with dark spots.

They look similar to brown trout, but the tail is slightly forked and not square.

There are no spots on the adipose fin of the Atlantic salmon.

When seagoing Atlantic salmon are in freshwater for more than forty-eight hours, they develop dark red spots alongside their original black spots and their belly flanks turn slightly pink in color.

The males develop an exaggerated upper jaw as they prepare to fight over females.

Atlantic Salmon

Regarded by many anglers as the only true salmon, the Atlantic salmon is a magnificent fish. The sea-run fish is extremely rare but the landlocked Atlantic salmon, also called the Ouananiche or Sebago salmon, is more plentiful.

Atlantic salmon are among the most acrobatic of all the game fish, making long powerful runs that can rapidly empty your reel. As Atlantic salmon rise well to a dry fly, fly-fishing for them is regarded by most anglers as the only sporting method of taking such magnificent fish.

Many anglers will only fish for Atlantic salmon and spend all their available free time in pursuit of the fish. Despite the fact that they make excellent food, anglers will very rarely keep a sea-run Atlantic salmon. The anadromous form of the Atlantic salmon species spawns in clear, coldwater streams, and then returns to the sea.

Unfortunately, factors like overfishing and environmental damage have made the anadromous Atlantic salmon an increasingly rare fish. This is despite the fact that the authorities involved in Atlantic salmon conservation have introduced significant measures to help the population grow. These include ladders to help the fish upstream, and the introduction of farmed fish into the wild population.

This is why most anglers try for the landlocked Atlantic salmon, whose numbers are not so threatened.

William Augenti with an Atlantic Salmon.

ATLANTIC SALMON

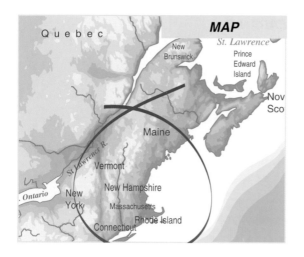

MAP

WHERE TO FISH

The anadromous form spawns in clear, coldwater streams along the North Atlantic coast, particularly in Maine, New England and Canada. Landlocked Atlantic salmon inhabit clear, coldwater lakes with gravelly inlet streams for spawning.

WHEN TO FISH

Fish for Atlantic salmon between April and November, when they are returning to the rivers where they spawn in the shallows in late fall.

FEEDING HABITS

Atlantic salmon eat mainly crustaceans, insects, and small fish. Interestingly, they do not feed once they're in the streams. Their willingness to take a fly is regarded purely as a reflex.

BEST BAIT

Anglers fly-fish for Atlantic salmon and there is an enormous amount of artificial flies on the market. Many anglers will make their own flies.

REMEMBER

Seagoing Atlantic salmon are a precious resource to be conserved so it's important to catch and release safely. Landlocked Atlantic salmon can be harvested for food.

WEIGHT

Seagoing Atlantic salmon will average between 8-12 lbs. Landlocked fish, particularly those grown commercially, will be heavier.

ATLANTIC SALMON

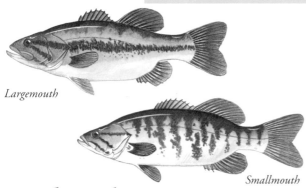

Largemouth

Smallmouth

Black Bass

Bass is the common name for several different fish but the name doesn't correspond to any specific scientific classification.

The most sought after freshwater bass is the black bass—both largemouth and smallmouth varieties. In Texas, varieties of bass also include the spotted and Guadalupe bass. Most freshwater bass are included within the sunfish family.

Some freshwater bass are also members of the seawater bass family. The black sea bass, also called the blackfish, is found on the Atlantic coast of America.

The major difference between largemouth and smallmouth bass is the length of the jaw. In the largemouth variety this extends to behind the eye.

Both fish have:

A light belly.

An uneven line of dark spots or bars extending along the flanks to the tail.

A spiny first dorsal fin, highest midway along, and soft second dorsal.

With the largemouth, the back is dark or black and the sides green or olive.

The smallmouth bass is golden brown.

Of the freshwater bass, the black bass is widely regarded as the best sport fish. They have a wide range, are very aggressive, and display great strength in the fight. Extremely active predators, they can be tempted to strike at pretty much any kind of bait or lure.

Largemouth bass were originally only native to southeastern Canada through the Great Lakes, as well as from the Mississippi valley (as shown on the map) to Mexico and Florida. From there, they ranged up the east coast to Maryland.

Largemouth bass have spread naturally, and, with the assistance of stocked rivers, today cover most states.

REMEMBER

When you're fishing in winter, look for differences in water color or temperature. These often produce a better bass bite.

BLACK BASS

WHERE TO FISH

The best places to look for largemouth bass are shallow lakes and the margins of rivers, where they stay in the weeded areas for food and safety. Smallmouth bass are found in warm rocky waters around twenty-five feet deep.

WHEN TO FISH

The best time to fish from shore is in winter around rocky areas because these warm up more quickly on sunny days. Access is better because the marginal undergrowth is not as thick as in summer.

FEEDING HABITS

Largemouth bass eat minnows, frogs, crayfish or crawdads, and insects. The smallmouth variety eats insect larvae, fish, and crayfish.

BEST BAIT

As they are such ferocious predators you can tempt bass to go for practically any kind of bait or lure. When bait fishing you can use worms, crayfish, leeches, or minnows. Artificial bait can include plastic worms and grubs, spoons, spinners, crank baits, and plugs. If you're fly-fishing, try artificials like bugs, streamers, poppers, and bucktails.

MAP

WEIGHT

Northern largemouth are rarely larger than 10 lbs but the southern largemouth can be more than 20 lbs in weight.

All bream are broadly similar: humpbacked with a spiny first dorsal fin and softer second dorsal. They all have a large anal spine.

The bluegill bream has a dark olive back, shading to a lighter belly.

As the name suggests, the redbreast has a red or crimson belly—although the same fish is called a yellowbelly in Texas.

Pumpkinseed bream are the flattest, most rounded of all the bream.

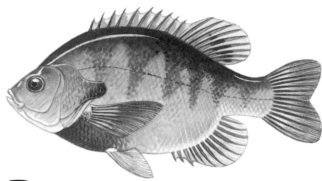

Bream

Although they are small, bream (pronounced "brim") are easy to catch and delicious to eat.

The most abundant bream in America are the bluegill, redbreast, and pumpkinseed. They are members of the sunfish family. Bream are common throughout the country and extend into Canada and Mexico.

They may be small fish, with most weighing under a pound, but bream often live in territory which is clogged with snags, roots, debris, and other obstacles. This means that it's a good idea to use a heavier line so you can work the fish through any debris. Lighter lines will simply snap.

REMEMBER

When fishing for bream of any kind, start in deeper water. Most anglers look for craters in the bottom and fish from the bank out to deep water, aiming to catch all the bream in a particular bedding area.

The reason for starting in deeper water is that hooked fish run from shallow to deeper water. If you fish in the shallows, any hooked fish will disturb others in the beds, making them increasingly reluctant to bite.

If you start catching bream in deep water first, they will move away from the bedding area, disturbing fewer fish and helping you to catch more.

Mike Sheldon with a Bluegill Bream.

MAP

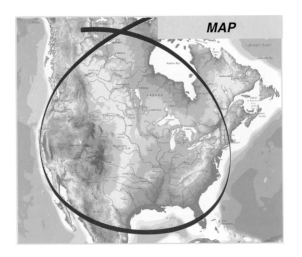

WEIGHT

Most bream are around 1 lb in weight, 2 lbs is good.

WHERE TO FISH

You can find bream in pretty much any kind of shallow water, from muddy ponds to clean rivers. Having said this, bream will move into deeper water in the winter.

WHEN TO FISH

You could try fishing for bream in winter when they've moved into the deeper drop-offs and the undergrowth in the denser margins is not so heavy.

FEEDING HABITS

Bream will eat anything although insects, worms, grubs, maggots, wasp larvae, and small minnows are their favorite foods.

BEST BAIT

You can catch bream using a wide variety of baits. The most common method is to use a small piece of worm or cricket suspended under a bobber. This inexpensive method is probably the oldest method of fishing. Apart from that, try nightcrawlers, red wigglers, mealworms, wax worms, crickets, horseflies, and other insects. As far as lures are concerned, use small artificial lures such as grubs, tiny spinners, or marabou jigs.

BREAM

Bullhead

The bullhead is actually a species of catfish and the one most commonly caught for food.

Broadly speaking, there are three types of bullhead recognized by the International Game Fish Association (IGFA) for records.

The black bullhead is found naturally from southern Ontario to the Gulf of Mexico between the Appalachian Mountains and Montana. It has also been introduced to Arizona, California, and other western states. There are a few bullheads east of the Appalachians.

◁ *Black bullheads have dark barbels and are uniformly dark with a light bar across the bar of their tail. They have between 15 and 21 anal fins and are usually around 6 to 10 inches long but can reach up to 18 inches.*

◁ *Brown bullheads are mottled in a pattern of brown and green with between 21 and 24 anal fins. They have dark lower barbels and more of a square tail than other bullheads.*

◁ *Yellow bullheads have whitish lower barbels, a rounded tail, and a long anal fin with between 24 and 27 rays.*

As they're catfish, bullhead also have sharp spines on their anal and dorsal fins that they raise to protect themselves. Contrary to popular belief, these spines are not poisonous.

Brown bullheads are native to eastern USA, both sides of the Appalachians. They have also been introduced widely across America, partly because they make excellent eating.

Yellow bullheads are also found naturally on both sides of the Appalachians but have been introduced into other areas. Record bullhead have been caught in Arizona.

WHERE TO FISH

When it comes to commercial fishing, bullhead found in the Mississippi River valley and the Gulf States are the most valuable.

Elsewhere, yellow bullhead live in deep, weedy lakes and slow streams. Brown bullhead also live in slow streams. Black bullhead inhabit shallow lakes and muddy streams.

WHEN TO FISH

Try fishing in late spring and summer when bullheads spawn in shallow depressions in sand or mud bottoms. In winter, bullhead look for deep water and protection from the current. Black bullhead are more common than the other species and are, therefore, the most popular for fishing.

FEEDING HABITS

Bullhead eat snails, crayfish, aquatic insects, other invertebrates, and small fish, as well as vegetation.

BEST BAIT

For live bait, use worms, shrimp, fish, large invertebrates, crustaceans, aquatic larvae, and grasshoppers. Otherwise, try liver, chicken, and stinkbait.

Like their close relative the channel catfish, bullhead are very rarely caught using lures.

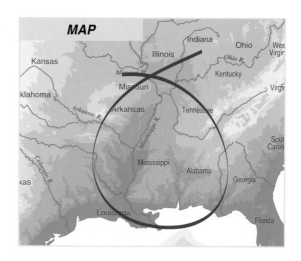

MAP

WEIGHT

A brown bullhead weighing 11 lbs was caught in Snohomish, Washington, in 2000.

There are many different types of carp, the majority have four barbels at the corners of their mouth, which is vacuum like.

They have a long concave dorsal fin with 20-26 rays.

The differences between the most common species are:

Common carp are covered with small, uniform scales.

Leather carp only have scales on their shoulders and back.

Mirror carp have a small number of large scales.

Liner carp are like mirror but have scales only along the lateral line.

Grass carp similar to the common but with a chub-shaped body and upturned mouth.

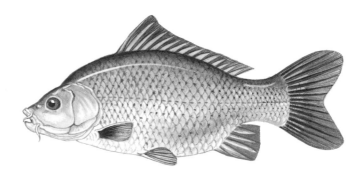

Carp

Wherever there are carp—anywhere in the world—they tend to inspire obsession among anglers.

The Carp Commission introduced carp into North America in 1876. Hundreds of the fish were brought into the country to be farmed as a food source. During 1879-1896 2.4 million carp were distributed, not only in America but also in parts of Canada, Costa Rica, Ecuador, and Mexico.

Today, as a result of anglers introducing them into just about every water in the continent, carp are everywhere.

REMEMBER

Carp are cunning and tremendously strong, which makes them a great sporting fish. They are pretty heavy, which can make them difficult when you handle them out of water. Once you have removed the hook, place the tip of your finger in the entrance of the mouth. This will keep the fish quite still.

Daniel Nally with a Grass Carp.

MAP

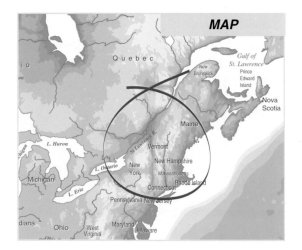

WHERE TO FISH

The trick is finding large fish that you can catch easily. The best places to start are small public waters. If the water is over ten years old, the carp will have reached a good size.

You can also find carp on the margins of a small lake or pond, where the food tends to be. If you're going after very large carp, head for rivers like the Connecticut, Potomac, and St. Lawrence Seaway. Thirty pound carp are regularly reported on these rivers.

WHEN TO FISH

Carp are especially active in the warmer months. If you're fishing a pond, try fishing with the wind in your face. Carp eventually migrate to the windward side because that's where the grubs and other protein sources are more available.

FEEDING HABITS

Adult carp are best suited to bottom fish and will eat anything, including snails, crayfish, blood worms, mussels, and shrimps.

WEIGHT

An 8 lb carp is a good catch for most anglers.

BEST BAIT

Carp have remarkably sensitive taste and sense receptors and will eat anything smelly. A rule of thumb is that carp will also tend to like whatever you do. Also try baits which use corn or oats that have fermented. They smell terrible but carp love them.

APPEARANCE

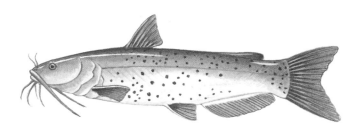

Catfish

Catfish is the common name for around 2,200 species of fish, with all but two species living in freshwater.

The name catfish comes from the feelers or barbels on each side of the upper, and sometimes lower, jaw of the fish, which suggest the whiskers of a cat.

Of the approximately 1,000 species of catfish found across North America, eleven are recognized for records by the International Game Fish Association.

Catfish appearances vary but the common features are:

◄ *A long muscular body with a small rounded tail.*

◄ *A large flat head.*

◄ *A huge mouth filled with tiny sharp teeth.*

◄ *Feelers at the corner of the top, and sometimes bottom, jaw.*

◄ *Sharp spines on the dorsal and pectoral fins.*

These are some of the most popular varieties of catfish:

Robby holding two Flathead Catfish.

• *Blue catfish:*
native to the Mississippi, Missouri and Ohio River basin systems in the USA and the largest of the American catfish.

• *Channel catfish:*
raised commercially, worldwide, as a sport and food fish and found in the wild all across North America.

• *Flathead catfish:*
probably the ugliest of all the cats, native to the Mississippi, Missouri, and Ohio basins and as far east as Lake Erie and Florida.

• *White catfish:* native to the east coast of America from Florida to New York and a popular game fish.

REMEMBER

The sharp spines at the leading edges of the dorsal and two pectoral fins of the catfish often sting careless anglers. When the fish is alarmed, it raises and locks the spike fins into an upright position.

Once you have learned where the spines are, it's as safe to hold a cat as it is any other fish.

WHERE TO FISH

Most catfish are scavengers. The best places to fish are in rivers, or wherever there is plenty of prey for the fish.

WHEN TO FISH

Fish on warm, humid, and overcast summer nights in the margins, using smelly bait.

FEEDING HABITS

The wide variety of catfish in North America causes feeding habits to vary. To give two examples:

- the flathead feeds on large numbers of other live fish;
- channel catfish feed on snails, crayfish, aquatic insects, other invertebrates, and small fish.

BEST BAIT

For live bait, use worms, shrimp, fish, large invertebrates, crustaceans, aquatic larvae, and grasshoppers. Otherwise, try liver, chicken, and stinkbait. But remember, flatheads only eat live fish and channel catfish are rarely caught using artificial lures.

MAP

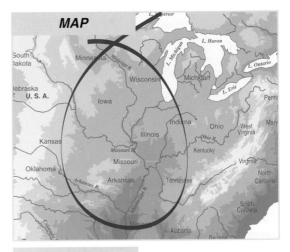

WEIGHT

Blue catfish weighing over 120 lbs have been caught using trotlines and bank hooks. Channel catfish can weigh up to 58 lbs. A flathead weighing 91 lbs 4 oz was caught on rod and reel, in Texas.

Black crappies are most often white or gray with dark gray or black spots covering most of their sides.

They have seven or eight dorsal spines.

White crappies are lighter, often have visible bars of gray extending down their sides, and have five or six dorsal spines.

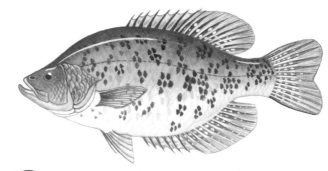

Crappie

Across North America, crappie are one of the most fun and best-tasting fish to catch.

Crappie is the common name for two species of fish found all over America, but mainly in the ponds and streams of the Mississippi valley and Great Lakes areas.

There are two sub-species of crappie: the black crappie, which gets its name from its slightly darker color, and the white crappie. Both of the sub-species have pretty much the same ways of feeding and spawning.

Some anglers claim that the black crappie prefers clearer water and the white crappie is more comfortable in muddier water.

Crappie swim in large schools. They prefer fairly warm water and you can normally find them in all types of cover. A fully-grown crappie averages 6-11 inches. With enough food, though, they can reach up to seventeen inches.

Jim Hollon holding a Black Crappie.

MAP

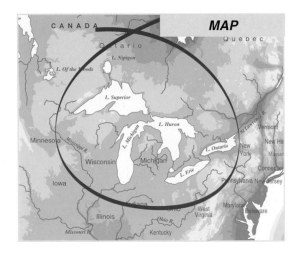

WHERE TO FISH

Whenever you're fishing for crappie, remember that they love structures. Look for areas with prominent cover like rock piles, shallow coves, stumps, points, and submerged brush.

Dedicated crappie anglers even create homes for big fish by sinking Christmas trees, old bushes, tires, and wooden palettes.

WHEN TO FISH

Crappie are pretty active all year round but the best times are fall and spring. Just before spawning—when the water reaches between 52 and 60 degrees—crappie feed aggressively in shallow water. This is called the pre-spawn period.

The female crappie lay their eggs in shallow water, which is then guarded by the males, before moving off into deeper water. So, if you catch smaller fish in shallow water, look for a deeper drop-off and you may find the females. When summer water cools down in the fall, crappie also feed heavily in order to fatten up for the winter.

WEIGHT

Most of the time, a crappie weighing between ½ and 1 lb is a good catch but, in certain circumstances, they can weigh up to 6 lbs. A large crappie is called a "slab."

BEST BAITS

The most popular bait for crappie has to be minnows and worms. The key thing with crappie is to match what the fish are eating.

You can also try marabou jigs, curly-tail grubs, or spinners, which are all very effective.

◁ *Lake whitefish are large, egg-shaped fish with small mouths.*

◁ *They are silvery white with backs that range from pale greenish brown to light or dark brown.*

◁ *The average length is 15 inches.*

◁ *Adult males often have a hump at the back of their head.*

Lake Whitefish

Lake whitefish are also known as common whitefish, Great Lakes whitefish, Sault whitefish, and humpback whitefish.

This species is regarded as very "plastic." Different populations in certain areas take on slightly different appearances. Some dwarf forms occur in northern lakes.

In the Great Lakes, lake whitefish can hybridize with ciscoes to produce a cross which is called mule whitefish. These grow faster and are a much brighter green than either parent. Lake whitefish also hybridize with inconnu.

Lake whitefish are not particularly great fighters and so don't provide a great deal of sport. They are becoming more and more popular however, especially with ice fishermen.

WHERE TO FISH

The best places to try for lake whitefish are the Great Lakes, Northwest Territories, and throughout Canada. As the name suggests, lake whitefish like cool, deep lakes although they have been found in slow-moving rivers.

WHEN TO FISH

Most anglers try for lake whitefish in winter. Try fly-fishing for lake whitefish on summer mornings and evenings when they come to the surface to feed.

FEEDING HABITS

Lake whitefish are mainly bottom feeders and eat insect larvae, molluscs, fish eggs, and small fish. During a hatch, you can often see them taking insects on the surface.

BEST BAIT

You can catch lake whitefish on small minnows, live or salted. Try using teardrop jigs baited with waxworms, and small jigging lures. Small lures should be used because their mouths are so small.

MAP

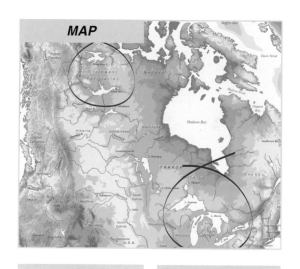

WEIGHT

15 lbs is average and 20 lbs is a good weight for lake whitefish.

REMEMBER

Lake whitefish have rather oily flesh but their flavor is excellent. You can eat them both fresh and smoked.

33

Muskie are often confused with Northern pike but it is easy to tell them apart.

Unlike the Northern pike, muskie have scales only on their upper cheek and gill cover.

They are also brown bodied with black spots or vertical bars (Northern pike markings are the reverse.)

There are usually between 12 and 18 pores on the underside of a muskie's jaw.

Muskellunge

The muskellunge, or muskie, is a powerful, elusive fish that is highly sought after by game anglers.

Muskie are found in the Great Lakes and the northeast. They are also known as lunge, maskinonge, great pike, and by over forty other names.

It is hard to predict how muskie are going to behave, which has made them a source of fascination for serious game anglers. Part of the fascination lies in the fact that very few are ever caught.

When they are hooked, muskie make a spectacular, but normally short, battle with victory in the muskie's favor. Their leaps and powerful runs most often break the line or straighten the angler's hook.

Muskie have been known to live for over thirty years. Females live longer than the males.

REMEMBER

A trophy muskie takes a long time to grow and will not quickly be replaced by a fish of an equal size. Sensible catch and release handling is the key to creating trophy fish.

Mac holding up a Musky

35

MAP

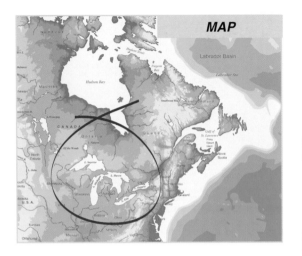

WHERE TO FISH

Muskie are extremely elusive, which is a major part of their appeal for serious game fishermen. Having said this, one of a muskie's favorite feeding habits is to wait in weed beds for its prey. So, it makes sense to look for this kind of habitat.

WHEN TO FISH

Like Northern pike, muskie become more lethargic the warmer the weather becomes. This is why it's best to fish for them in cooler weather.

FEEDING HABITS

Muskie will eat whatever they find, although fish are their favorite food. They will eat frogs, crayfish, muskrats, and ducklings. Ideally, muskie prefer large items of food and their growth is slow if these are not available.

A muskie's method of feeding is to wait for its prey in weed beds, lunge forward and sink in its large, tooth-lined jaws. The victim, dead or stunned, is gulped down head first.

WEIGHT

A 30 lbs muskie will have taken between fourteen and seventeen years to grow. The world record is 69 lbs 15 oz for a fish caught in the St Lawrence River, New York, in 1957.

BEST BAIT

Muskie fishermen commonly use bait fish weighing a pound or more with foot-long plugs and spinners. The best way to catch muskie that you want to release is to use artificial bait. Muskie anglers always use stout baitcasting rods and 30 to 50 lbs quality line with a wire leader.

Although very similar to muskie, the following characteristics are unique to the Northern pike:

◄ *Light markings on a dark background.*

◄ *Lower cheeks that are completely scaled.*

◄ *Five or fewer pores on each side of the underside of the jaw.*

Northern Pike

Known as the "alligator of the north," the Northern pike is a very popular fish with game anglers.

Northern pike are popular because, quite simply, they are reasonably easy to catch. They are large, extremely predatory—always willing to strike the right lure or bait—and somewhat slow. Another reason Northern pike are prized is because they make good eating. Their chunky white fillets are every bit as good as walleye.

As Northern pike often share waters with muskie, a close relative, a hybrid of the two, called the tiger muskie has evolved. It is most often infertile and shares the characteristics of both parents.

Clarence Kalkofen holding a Northern Pike.

REMEMBER

The quickest way to tell a Northern pike from a muskie is by the markings. Northerns have light markings on a dark body and muskies the reverse.

WHERE TO FISH

Northern pike are found in the Great Lakes and all over the northeast. In Minnesota, they live in all the state's lakes and streams. In the Mississippi valley they coexist with muskie. Small Northern pike remain in shallow, weedy water all year round while larger fish move into deeper waters throughout the summer.

WHEN TO FISH

If you're after large Northern pike, there's little point trying to catch them in warm weather as they become lethargic. They eat very little and will sometimes lose weight. The best time to fish is when the water turns cooler and they begin to forage for prey.

FEEDING HABITS

Intent on conserving energy, Northern pike focus on large prey, often swallowing fish a third their size. Common food includes yellow perch, tullibee, suckers, minnows, and other Northern pike. They will also eat sunfish and bass, as well as leeches, frogs, and crayfish.

BEST BAIT

The best lures are big spoons, spinners, and jerkbaits but Northern pike will attack any artificial lure that looks worth eating. An effective bait is a large minnow fished beneath a float. Northern pike, once hooked, typically leap or thrash about on the water surface before making a series of powerful runs.

MAP

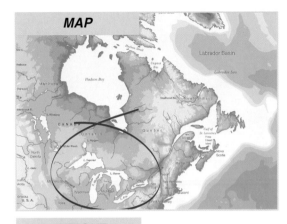

WEIGHT

Northern pike are around 2 lbs, although trophy fish of over 20 lbs are caught every year. They grow faster in the south than the north. The world record for Northern pike currently stands at 55 lbs.

There are five main sub-species of Pacific salmon:

Chinook salmon: *highly prized, black gums, silver spotted tail, lightly spotted blue-green back.*

Sockeye salmon: *almost toothless, silver blue, great number of long gill rakers, bulging glassy eyes.*

Coho salmon: *bright blue, metallic blue dorsal surface, wide tail base, white gums, black tongue, a few spots on the upper portion of their bodies, silver-colored tails.*

Pink salmon: *tiny scales, tail heavily marked with large oval spots.*

Chum salmon: *white tip on the anal fin, silvery sides.*

Pacific Salmon

Of the two main salmon species in North America, the Pacific salmon is by far the most prolific fish in the wild.

The numbers of Atlantic salmon, regarded as the true salmon, in the wild have been dramatically reduced by overfishing and pollution.

Salmon are found in both fresh and saltwater in the colder regions of North America. They often return from salt to freshwater to breed and the young migrate back to freshwater after they mature.

The salmon's migratory instinct is extraordinary. Each generation spawns in exactly the same place as the generation before. Species that don't migrate always breed in the same stream. Pacific salmon only spawn once before dying.

You should follow these steps when releasing a fish back into the wild:
- *Be careful not to knock off any scales.*
- *Use a hook releaser such as long-nose pliers or a gaff.*
- *Sacrifice your hook when necessary.*
- *Revive fish gently.*
- *Reduce your chance of hooking small fish by using large lures or artificial baits.*
- *If you're fishing from a boat, release the fish without taking them out of the water.*

Dave Smith with a Coho Salmon.

MAP

WHERE TO FISH

You can fish for Pacific salmon all over North America, as far north as Alaska and down to Oregon, Idaho, and Washington State.

WHEN TO FISH

The most popular fishing resorts have year-round fishing. At the Campbell River on Vancouver Island, British Columbia, anglers fish the winter springs from December to mid-March. In April, they fish for mature salmon coming down from Alaska. Chinook bound for the Columbia River in Oregon pass through the channel in June. Chum salmon provide the best fishing from September to December.

WEIGHT

The largest of the Pacific salmon, the chinook is usually sold at market weighing around 20 lbs, but specimens of over 100 lbs have been recorded. The smallest of the species is the pink salmon.

FEEDING HABITS

Salmon usually eat smaller fish, crustaceans, and insects.

BEST BAIT

Anglers fish for salmon using a wide variety of artificial flies and a rod and reel. If you're going after specimen fish, use larger bait like fish.

PACIFIC SALMON

◀ Steelhead are very similar to rainbow trout in appearance.

◀ When they are out at sea, they are a uniform color.

◀ As they come back to freshwater to spawn, their red stripe and spotted back appears.

Steelhead

Regarded by many anglers as the most exciting sporting fish to try for, steelhead are notoriously difficult to catch.

The anadromous cousin of rainbow trout, steelhead are very different both in behavior and size. In the Great Lakes, for instance, steelhead can be between two and ten times the size of most rainbow trout.

43

One of the most migratory of all freshwater fish in the USA, steelhead can travel thousands of miles in their lifetime. Steelhead in the Great Lakes will start their life in the stream, head to the Great Lakes to forage and grow up and then return to the stream to spawn. After they have spawned they return to the Lakes and start all over again.

Ralph Jenkins holding up a Steelhead.

WHERE TO FISH

Steelhead are found all over the northwest. They tend to stay in the tailouts of pools, in runs that are between three and six feet deep and anywhere that fast and slow currents meet. You may also find them at the shallower edges of deep pools and at the mouths of tributary streams.

Wherever there is cover, such as a large rock, it will be used by steelhead—bankside log jams, for instance. You will not be likely to find steelhead in white water or the bottom of deep pools.

WHEN TO FISH

Summer-run steelhead will enter rivers from June through to September. As the water rises and warms in March and April, there will be plenty of fish in the rivers.

FEEDING HABITS

Remember that cold winter currents will slow the steelhead's metabolism, which means that you will need to fish the deeper runs. Steelhead will eat small fish but they also feed on plankton, insects, and crustaceans.

MAP

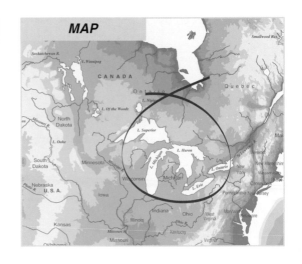

BEST BAIT

The best baits for steelhead are ghost shrimp, mud shrimp, and salmon roe. You can use just about any lure on a steelhead but you could try imitation eggs, nymphs, and streamers.

WEIGHT

The average weight for steelhead is between 8 and 12 lbs but fish as large as 42 lbs have been recorded. They are usually between 1 ft 8 in. and 2 ft 6 in. long.

Rainbow trout are often very beautiful. ▶

They have spotted backs. ▶

Look for a red stripe across the side, which is especially pronounced when they move into freshwater streams to spawn. ▶

Rainbow Trout

Whether you're an angler or not, there is no finer sight to see than a leaping rainbow trout.

Among anglers, the leaping ability of the rainbow is legendary. When hooked, a rainbow nearly always shoots straight out of the water, often several times, before coming to the net.

The rainbow is native to the lakes and streams of western America. Their fighting spirit and delicate flavor, have led to them being introduced worldwide.

Rainbow trout are a particular fly-fishing favorite because they are less wary than other trout—brown trout for instance—and more likely to bite.

REMEMBER

The size of a rainbow trout depends very much on the habitat. If you're catching fish to eat, this probably doesn't make much difference but if you're going after the really big fish, head for a large lake.

Dale Daneman with a Rainbow Trout.

MAP

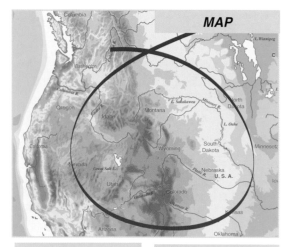

WHERE TO FISH

There are many specialist rainbow trout fishing areas in the lakes and streams of western America, to which the fish is native. If you especially want to land big fish, try large lakes where you know there is plenty of food for the fish. If you can, try to avoid densely populated areas where many anglers will have tried for rainbow trout.

WHEN TO FISH

Like steelhead, rainbow trout will enter rivers from June through to September. As the water rises and warms in March and April, there will be plenty of fish in the rivers.

Once again, remember that cold winter currents will slow the rainbow's metabolism. This means that you will need to fish the deeper runs.

WEIGHT

The size of a rainbow trout depends on the availability of food in the stream and the water temperature. In some streams, they may routinely weigh only 1 lb but in a lake with plenty of food they may reach as much as 33 lbs.

BEST BAIT

Although rainbow trout are normally fished for using a fly, they can also be caught on spinners, spoons, plugs, and a wide variety of bait. Baits include anything from worms to marshmallows.

FEEDING HABITS

Rainbow trout chiefly eat immature and adult insects, plankton, crustaceans, fish eggs, and small fish. Fly-fishing is particularly effective with rainbow trout because of their habit of taking adult insects on the surface.

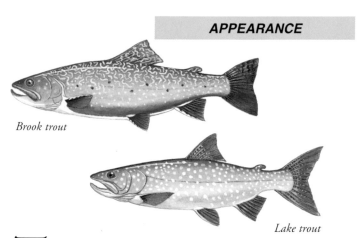

Brook trout

Lake trout

▸ Brook trout are greenish-brown with red spots and marks, like waves, on their backs.

▸ The male has a red band on its sides, and during spawning develops a hooked jaw and red belly.

▸ Male fins may turn deep orange with black and white highlights.

▸ Lake trout are able to change their color slightly to camouflage themselves.

Trout: *Brook and Lake*

Brook and lake trout are prized by anglers both as a game fish and because they are delicious to eat.

Brook trout are not great leapers but are very powerful fighters for their size. They are also regarded as better fish to eat than either brown or rainbow trout.

Lake trout do not leap at all. Instead they wage a strong, long, and determined battle under water.

WHERE TO FISH

You'll find brook trout in streams, lakes, and ponds that are not too cold or clear, or at the headwaters of spring-fed streams. The best brook trout waters are in regions of Labrador, Quebec and Manitoba, which are not well populated. Lake trout like cold, clear, well-oxygenated lakes, which is where they are almost exclusively found.

WHEN TO FISH

Brook trout are slow-growing compared to most other trout and tend to overpopulate their habitat. They then become stunted. Lake trout prefer water ranging from 40°F to 52°F in temperature. In spring and fall, you can find them at depths of around twenty feet.

FEEDING HABITS

Items found in brook trout stomachs have included small larval insects and fish, field mice, and even snakes. Lake trout normally eat small fish like ciscoes, smelt, or sculpins. In some lakes they eat nothing but plankton, insects, and crustaceans.

MAP

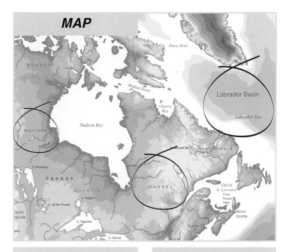

BEST BAIT

Brook trout will take a dry fly but you will have better luck with subsurface flies. Many fish are caught on small spoons and spinners. Worms, leeches, and minnows are all good live bait. Most lake trout are caught by trolling with spoons or minnow-like plugs attached to wire-line rigs or downriggers.

WEIGHT

Although the largest brook trout on record weighed 14 lbs 8 oz, they only average about 2 lbs.

The world record for a lake trout caught on a gillnet is a staggering 102 lbs.

Walleye have olive-green sides with gold flecks.

The dorsal fin is spiny and has no spots but a black rear base.

A walleye's tail has a white tip on its lower lobe.

Walleye

Other names for walleye include walleyed pike, pickerel, jackfish, dore, and ol' marble eyes.

Walleye are highly prized by anglers for several reasons. They stay deep, and are strong fighters which put up a determined fight. Handsome fish, they are also excellent for eating.

The walleye is named for its pearlescent eye which is caused by a layer of pigment in the retina called the "tapetum lucidum". This makes their eyes extremely light sensitive and means that they are comfortable feeding at night or in murky water.

Philip Edison holding a Walleye.

REMEMBER

Sauger is a close cousin of the walleye and the two are often difficult to tell apart. You need to look at the tip of the tail, which is white on a walleye but not on a sauger.

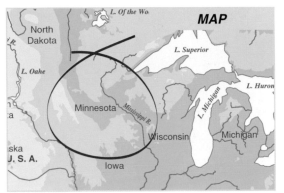

MAP

In Minnesota alone, anglers catch around 3.5 million walleye totaling two thousand tons every year, which is why they are a carefully managed fish.

WEIGHT

The average walleye weighs just over 1 lb. Having said this, the world record, set in 1960, is 25 lbs, caught in Old Hickory Lake, Tennessee.

WHERE TO FISH

Walleye are most common in large, windswept natural lakes that are only moderately or not particularly clear. They are also found in smaller lakes, reservoirs, rivers, and streams with a gentle current. Clean, hard bottoms, and water temperature from 65°F to 75°F are preferred.

WHEN TO FISH

As walleye have light-sensitive eyes, they bite best around dusk and dawn, at night or in cloudy weather.

FEEDING HABITS

Walleye are mainly fish eaters but they also feed on immature and adult aquatic insects, leeches, crayfish, snails, and larval salamanders. Except where they are in murky waters, the fish feed most heavily in dim-light periods, especially when light is rapidly fading.

BEST BAIT

Walleye are often caught with baits and lures that include nightcrawlers, leeches, jigs, spinners, and minnow plugs.

WALLEYE

White Sturgeon

The white sturgeon is the largest and most powerful fish in North American inland waters.

Most white sturgeon are anadromous and spend the bulk of their time in the estuaries of large rivers along the Pacific coast, entering coastal rivers to spawn. Some, though, spend their whole lives in the upper reaches of these rivers, hundreds of miles away from the sea.

White sturgeon are excellent to eat, with firm, white meat. Their eggs make good caviar. A typical white sturgeon rig is a heavy saltwater rod, a 100-lb test line, a ¾ lb singer, and a 12/0 hook.

The upper half of the white sturgeon's body is gray to brown, usually speckled with white.

The lower half is pale gray to white.

A white sturgeon's snout is rather flat and blunt when seen from above.

The barbels are closer to the tip of the snout than those of a lake sturgeon.

White sturgeon live for a remarkably long time. The largest fish are probably one hundred years old.

WHITE STURGEON

WHERE TO FISH

White sturgeon are normally found in rivers with clean water and a moderate current.

WHEN TO FISH

The best time to fish for white sturgeon is in the evening when they feed most heavily.

FEEDING HABITS

White sturgeon are predominantly bottom feeders but they eat a wider variety of food than other sturgeon. As well as insect larvae, crustaceans, and fish eggs, they eat dead and live fish, frogs, and clams. The stomach of one large sturgeon is rumored to have contained a domestic cat.

BEST BAIT

Cut fish, shrimp, and large clusters of nightcrawlers are all excellent for catching white sturgeon.

MAP

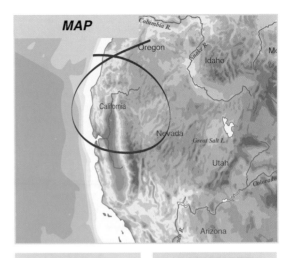

WEIGHT

Sturgeon can grow very large. Although the world record of 488 lbs is for a fish caught in the Carquinez Straits, California, far larger fish have been caught commercially.

REMEMBER

White sturgeon feed late in the day so that is the best time to fish for them.

Golden body color—
males are more brightly
colored than females.

Humped back.

Longer body shape than
the white perch.

Six to nine boldly-striped
dark bars for camouflage.

Orange ventral and anal
fins that become bright
orange on males in the
breeding season.

Big mouth and
large eyes.

Yellow Perch

There are around one hundred and fifty species of bony fish called perch, characterized by two dorsal fins that are separate or only joined narrowly.

Perch are found both in fresh and saltwater. The common perch is found across Europe and northern Asia and is greenish with dark, vertical bars on its sides for camouflage.

In the USA, species of perch include the white and yellow perch, which is the most common.

Yellow perch—or the striped, raccoon, or jack perch—are originally only native to North America, east of the Rocky Mountains and Atlantic Coast watersheds south to South Carolina. They have also been introduced across the country and are distributed throughout Pennsylvania.

More recently, yellow perch have spread further across the USA, traveling in schools that can be as large as two hundred fish. During the day, the schools stay in deeper, darker water and move closer to the shallows to feed later in the day.

Yellow perch are popular with open-water anglers and ice fishermen.

REMEMBER

Perch are one of the best freshwater fish for eating, with firm and tasty white, flaky meat.

Mark Berg holding up a Yellow Perch.

YELLOW PERCH

MAP

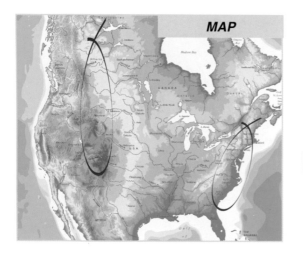

WHERE TO FISH

If you're looking for large yellow perch, try the open water areas of large lakes with reasonably clear water, a firm bottom, and sparse or moderate vegetation. Smaller perch are found in small lakes, ponds, and sluggish streams. Yellow perch are rarely found in water more than thirty feet deep.

WHEN TO FISH

Small perch, in particular, are often the first fish caught by freshwater anglers because they're not usually very cautious. They're also not very strong fighters so are not particularly satisfying sport fish.

Yellow perch normally feed during daylight and hardly ever at night. They are active all year round, including under the ice. This makes them a favorite with ice anglers who catch them using jigging rods and tip-ups.

FEEDING HABITS

Perch feed most actively during daylight and their food includes immature aquatic insects, crayfish, snails, small fish, and fish eggs. Adult fish will eat smaller perch.

WEIGHT

Yellow perch don't usually weigh more than a couple of pounds although the world record weight is 4 lbs 3 oz for a fish caught in New Jersey in 1865. Growth will depend on habitat.

BEST BAIT

The most popular baits used for yellow perch are small minnows, worms, leeches, crickets, grubs, and crayfish tails. Small jigs and spinners are the lures that get the best results.

YELLOW PERCH

Particular Species

Many of the freshwater fish described in this book can be found all over large areas of North America, but here are a few good spots for some of the fish mentioned.

LOCATIONS

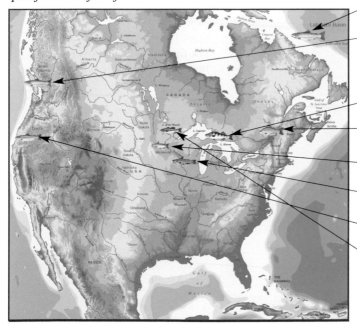

Atlantic salmon—
Labrador

Pacific salmon—
Queen Charlotte Island, British Columbia

Yellow perch—
Great Lakes

Carp—
St Lawrence River

Black bullhead—
Mississippi River

Channel catfish—
Red River, Minnesota

Steelhead—
Rogue River, Oregon

Bass—
Lake of the Woods, Canada

61

PARTICULAR SPECIES

Worldwide

Many dedicated anglers take fishing vacations all over the world in pursuit of their chosen quarry. These are some of the favored destinations and the fish you can find there.

MAP

BRITAIN

Angling in Britain is extremely sophisticated, with a wide variety of techniques being employed to catch fish. British fish share many of the same names as North American fish but are totally different species.

Apart from trout and salmon fly-fishing, the main reason anglers visit Britain is to fish for carp. The main varieties of carp in Britain are wild, common, mirror, leather, and crucian. They can be found all over the country but serious carp anglers head for still waters.

The best time to go fishing for carp in Britain is in the summer months.

FRANCE

France is excellent for catfish and carp. Serious catfish anglers vacationing in France head for: the one hundred miles stretch of the river Saône from Lyon to Chalon; the river Loire between Decize and Gien; Lake Cassien is excellent for carp but Salagou and St Quivox are also worth a visit. The River Seine has produced some large specimen carp.

SPAIN

Spain is a popular destination for catfish anglers. Plenty of enormous fish have been pulled out of the river Ebro.

RUSSIA

Serious catfish anglers head for Eastern Europe. The rivers Desna and Volga in Russia have often produced monster catfish, weighing up to 400 lbs. As most anglers will be aware, this part of the world can be somewhat volatile. It's important to be extremely careful and take advice from people who know the area if you're planning a visit.

MAPS

MAPS

AFRICA

The Zambezi river is home to the tiger fish, prized by fly-fishermen. Although locals have always spun for them with an artificial lure, the real challenge is to land one using a fly. Tiger fish are reported to be the hardest-fighting freshwater fish.

Tiger fish are a brilliant tarnished silver, flanked by horizontal bars with bright orange and red fins. With razor-sharp teeth protruding from their lips, they're a fearsome predator.

Although most fish are about 3-6 lbs, the depths of the river are home to fish weighing 15 lbs. When you take a tiger, their reaction is explosive. They leap and twist with power way beyond their size.

INDIA

Masheer inhabit the rivers of India and Nepal. They are a sub-species of carp and mainly bottom feeders. They have huge appetites and will reliably rise to a fly or spoon before exploding with aggression. Growing to over 100 lbs in size, and with enormous strength, masheer will haul anglers along the river bank.

BRAZIL

Brazil's Amazon basin is home to one of the fiercest freshwater fighting fish, the fire peacock bass. Probably the most colorful of all the game species, the fish is bright red on the underbelly with golden flanks distinctively marked with three "peacock eyes" and a huge mouth.

Fire peacock bass cruise the shallow and fallen logs along the banks of lagoons and will readily take a fly. Once they do, they're capable of ripping a rod from the hands of an unsuspecting angler with the first strike. From then on, the fish make short, deep, unstoppable runs.

Thomas Wäscher with a Peacock Bass.

As well as the fire peacock bass, you'll find the traira, micuda, matrinxa, jacunda, triara, pacu, payara, jau and, of course, the legendary piranha.

MAP

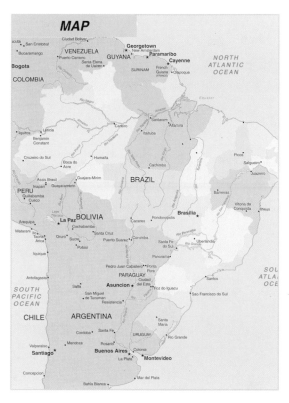

MAP

ARGENTINA

Argentina is a popular destination for game anglers seeking trophy size sea-run brown trout.

Brown, rainbow, and brook trout were first introduced to the country in the 1930s by keen British anglers. Competition for food was so intense that the fish migrated downstream to the southern Atlantic Ocean to feed on the rich supplies.

Well fed, they return to the rivers to spawn from November to April. There are no natural predators and only limited pressure from commercial fishing so the numbers of fish and average size have steadily increased.

Due to a strict catch and release policy, fish over 20 lbs are not uncommon and there are stories of fish weighing over 30 lbs.

The most famous river to fish is the Rio Grande but the Rio Gallegos is also excellent.

AUSTRALIA

The Murray cod, or goodoo, is Australia's most famous freshwater fish. It's a monster, with the record fish weighing in at 250 lbs and measuring over six feet long.

Murray cod were originally extremely common until the early part of the 20th century. Today, they're found anywhere from small, clear rocky streams to large, slow-flowing rivers with lots of deep holes, fallen trees, stumps, clay banks, and overhanging vegetation—but only within the Murray-Darling river areas.

Virtually anything that moves is fair game for a Murray cod, including other fish, spiny freshwater crayfish, shrimp, freshwater mussels, frogs, water fowl, small mammals, tortoises, and other reptiles.

Specialists going after Murray cod use relatively heavy tackle. When they're aiming for larger fish, line-breaking strain of over 50 lbs is not uncommon. If they're trolling in heavy cover, where the fish are found, super braided lines are used. Many Murray cod specialists, fish using only large trolled

MAP

bait or cast deep-diving lures with a wide action at dead slow speed. At night surface lures like large flies work.

Murray cod have been caught on baits as diverse as rabbits and hard-boiled eggs but the most common baits are bardi grubs, yabbies, shrimps, and scrub worms.

Tackle

Depending on the fish you're going after and the water conditions, there are many different methods of freshwater fishing. There are a wide variety of baits and all kinds of specialist equipment to experiment with.

This is all part of the pleasure of angling, of course. But it's vital to make certain when you're buying potentially expensive equipment—a British rod, for instance—that it does what you want it to comfortably. It should also give you plenty of enjoyment.

With a rod, for example, it's important to consider what you're fishing for, how far you need to cast, and what line strength and casting weights you need.

REMEMBER

As tackle is becoming more and more sophisticated and correspondingly expensive, the last thing you want to do is treat it badly.

Rubbing candle wax on rod joints to prevent sticking.

LOOKING AFTER YOUR TACKLE

It's safe to say that you'll get more pleasure out of angling if your tackle is kept clean, neat, and well looked after.

For instance, you don't want to spend hours untangling long, knotted lengths of line or rooting around for weights in the bottom of your tackle box.

CLEANING

It's surprising how many anglers don't bother to clean their rods. Wiping your rods down with a cloth and soapy water after you've used them and regularly replacing worn rings is vital.

TAKING CARE OF YOUR ROD

A good way to prevent the joints of your rod sticking together is to rub candle wax on the male section. This is the part of the rod that fits inside the hollow end of the next length of rod.

If your rod ever gets stuck together, it's extremely difficult to pull the sections apart by yourself. Ask another angler to help you. Both of you grip the rod on one side of the joint with one hand and the other side of the joint with the other.

With both of you pulling steadily, it shouldn't be too difficult to get the rod apart.

Through

Progressive

Fast taper

REMEMBER

If you are fishing seriously, you should have a selection of rods for different circumstances. It makes sense to live with one rod for a while and expand your range gradually.

There are three basic types of rod action:

◄ **Through:** *for a uniform smooth curve when playing a fish.*

◄ **Progressive:** *rods that give more backbone and increasing power buildup in the butt to control larger fish.*

◄ **Fast taper:** *these are very stiff in the butt and have extremely flexible tips, designed for long casting and picking up the line.*

69

Centerpin

Fixed Spool

Multiplying

RODS

In other parts of the world, Britain especially, there is an enormous variety of rods to choose from—reflecting the more complex fishing conditions in these countries. A typical fishing equipment catalog might list as many as twenty-five different styles. These may range from inexpensive graphite-fiberglass quivertips to an elaborate combination and graphite rod.

Such sophistication is not really necessary for most North American fishing, unless you're specializing in something like big game fish or trout.

REELS

If you're ledgering, in particular, you should have at least one of each of the basic types of reel:

- *Fixed spool:* the most common type of reel.
- *Centerpin:* for trotting and ledgering certain fish.
- *Closed face:* for difficult conditions and strong winds.
- *Multipliers:* use when you're trotting for big fish, like catfish, for example, and need a large amount of heavy line.

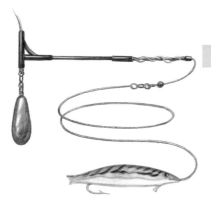

Downriggers are excellent for lake fishing in summer when you're trolling—fishing from a boat—and coldwater fish like lake trout have gone into the depths. They give such obvious advantages that it's surprising they're not used more often.

A downrigger allows you to control the depth of the bait you're using when trolling. It consists of a reel of small, steel cable, usually 150-300 ft of 150 lbs test, which runs through a pulley at the end of a boom. This is usually between one and five feet long.

With a downrigger, you can use light-action rods and lines for the kind of fight that you won't get with other deep trolling methods. You can fish deeper with more speed than is usual. It's also much easier to run multiple lines on the same boat without tangles.

Downriggers range from cheaper manual models—starting at around fifty dollars—to electric and extremely sophisticated electronic models. These will tell you the depth of the water and follow the contour of the bottom.

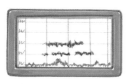

FISHFINDERS

Fishfinders are used by serious anglers, particularly sports anglers. If you use a fishfinder, you want one that has the power to show fish even when they're very deep. Once you know how deep the fish are, you know how far to send down the downriggers.

A dual-angle fishfinder, with a wide angle, is also useful because it lets you see your downrigger weights. This way you can adjust your baits to the level of the fish.

LINES

Modern filament lines are produced to a very high standard, with remarkably narrow diameters and dramatically increased breaking strain. Some of the new fluorocarbon lines are almost invisible in water.

Whatever you're using as your main line, change it regularly. All lines deteriorate over time, especially if they're exposed to the sun. Lines ought to be renewed three times every season.

FLOATS

When float fishing, it's important to make certain that the float you choose is right for the job. Floats used in rivers will be heavier, higher up the stem for stability and riding a current. The weight in stillwater floats is lower down to counter the effects of drift.

You also need to weight your float correctly for maximum sensitivity.

LURES

Lures imitate the behavior of the prey of predatory fish. Most predators react strongly to violent movement and vibration, which are the factors behind lure design and use.

There is an enormous range of lures on the market. This is a brief sample of the range of one inch flatfish lures offered by one manufacturer:

1. Black/silver flake
2. Chartreuse
3. Orange fluorescent
4. Frog
5. Fluorescent red
6. Tequila polka dot

Standard hook   Wire hook

REMEMBER

If you're ledgering for very cautious fish, use a wire hook but remember it will have a short lifespan. Try a wire hook with a slight outpoint—this will make it more efficient.

HOOKS

European manufacturers make a wide variety of hooks but, unless you're going after highly specialized fish, all you really need is a good-quality, sharp hook.

Bait

As you would imagine, with such a wide variety of fishing available in North America, there is a correspondingly extensive choice of bait.

REDWORMS

These are extremely effective and simple to find and keep.
To look for worms, go out onto close-cropped grass two hours after dark on a calm night following steady rain. Pull the worm gently out of its hole without breaking it—broken worms don't survive.

If you want to make sure you have a good supply of redworm, make a compost heap of grass cuttings, leaves, kitchen waste, and animal manure. Keep your worms in moist soil with damp moss.

MAGGOTS

The most popular maggots are the large grubs of the big bluebottle meat fly. You can use pinkies, which are greenfly larvae, and housefly larvae.

Bluebottle maggots are the most common hookbait. Pinkies and housefly larvae can be used as hookbait but are more commonly particle attractors in groundbaits or for swimfeeders.

Castors are maggots in the chrysalis stage. They're among the most effective baits for all freshwater at all times of the year,

particularly when combined with hemp. You can use them with a swimfeeder.

BREAD

Bread is one of the most versatile baits. If you're using bread crust as bait, make sure it's very tough. For hookbait, tear off a piece of crust with a good chunk of bread attached.

Mashed bread is used for looser feeding. Handfuls of fresh, squeezed breadcrumbs will keep a swim primed. Liquidized bread is even more attractive to fish and more economical.

MEAT

There are a variety of different meats you can use for bait, including dogmeat.

One of the most widely used meats is any kind of cold cut. Remember that this becomes unappealing to fish if it's been left on a hook all day and if there have been no bites, change it regularly.

You can also try sausage meats and spicy sausage, which can be used on their own or as part of a paste. Try prepared sausage like pepperoni, salami, and bologna.

REMEMBER

Although shrimps make an excellent bait they're fragile and can be expensive.

Bread

Meat

Cheese

Hemp

Synthetic

PASTES

Pastes are extremely versatile, whether you make them yourself or buy them ready-made. Making your own paste means you can experiment until you arrive at the right consistency.

Bread paste is cheap, easy to make, and effective.

Meat paste is made with sausage meat, finely chopped canned foods, or soft pet food and mixed with breadcrumbs, biscuit meal, or soybean flour.

Cheese paste is great for fish like carp. Make it by mixing Cheddar, Danish Blue, and frozen pastry mix, folding them in together.

SYNTHETIC PASTES

Hemp paste is good for taking certain fish, including carp. To make hemp paste, crush hemp and mix with shortcrust pastry. Use water or eggs and a commercial mix for your base. Add liquid or powdered flavors, colors or sweeteners. These can be curry or cheese powder, powdered crayfish or mussel.

REMEMBER

Chocolate

You can also try ingredients like canned meat or fish with a bulk-binding agent. Believe it or not, chocolate bars mixed with breadcrumbs get good results.

BAIT OILS

For carp, you can also try bait dips, which come in flavors such as corn, anise, garlic, and crayfish.

There are many sophisticated bait oils or sauces on the market that make your bait even more attractive to fish. For instance, crayfish bait which is used for catfish, and shrimp oil for steelhead.

The newer fish oil emulsions are excellent. Unlike traditional fish oils which stay on the surface, these sink to the bottom like a rock, break up and crawl along the bottom sending out a heavy scent trail to the bait. Try them when you're fishing for carp.

PARTICLE BAITS

Many fish like large quantities of food, or particles, or bloodworm colonies. You can get the same effect by saturating a small area with a large number of particles.

Particle baits should also be big enough to be used on their own, or with two or three others on a big hook. Sweetcorn is the classic particle bait because it attracts just about any freshwater fish. You can also try hempseed, chick peas, or tiger nuts.

Mass bait glued to a hook

A boilie, floating bait

Boilies

MASS BAITS

The more bait you use, the better chance you have of attracting fish. Individual pieces of mass bait need to be a lot smaller than particle bait. You can use hempseed, dari, tares, wheat, and pearl barley. Mass baits can be glued to a large hook.

FLOATING BAITS

Used to attract surface-feeding fish, floating baits include boilies converted to floaters by baking them, high protein floaters, floating pet foods, bread crust, and worms.

BOILED BAITS

"Boilies" are an integral part of carp fishing, particularly in Britain. There are plenty of excellent commercial boilies available but specialists prefer to make their own.

You can either add your own ingredients to a commercially available base or make your own. Use birdseed, mixed ground nuts, fish meals, milk products, or a combination.

PREBAITING/GROUNDBAITING

Prebaiting is preparing a swim with bait hours, days, and sometimes weeks before fishing. Groundbaiting means introducing bait or creating a feed carpet before or during a session.

In North America, this technique is not particularly common and is actually illegal in some states. But it gets results, particularly when it's used for match fishing.

Groundbaiting, creating a feed carpet using bread

The most simple type of groundbait is bread but there are a wide range of varieties commercially available.

Groundbait is used to attract fish, carry other feed baits into the swim, and hold fish near the hookbait. The type and consistency of groundbait—from cloudy through to heavy and binding—will vary according to conditions.

For instance, cloudy groundbaits are normally used in still waters where they also pull fish up off the bottom.

Slingshot

REMEMBER

Groundbait is very light so don't struggle to throw it great distances. It's better to learn to use a slingshot.

A torch
For when you're
fishing at night.

Scissors and penknife
These are essential
pieces of kit for plenty
of different reasons.

Slingshot
If you're fishing in a state
that allows chumming or
pre-feeding, you'll need a
slingshot for baiting.

Depth plumb
A depth plumb is
a useful way to
establish where your
quarry's feeding.

Guy ropes, and bivvie pegs
If you want to record
your catch you'll need
to have guy ropes and
bivvie pegs to keep it in
deep water.

Tackle Box Items

*There are certain things any angler needs to keep in a
well-equipped tackle box.*

Line *Shot* *Weights*

Line, shot, weights, and a dispenser
You need plenty of spare line, non-toxic shot
ranging from small to large and a dispenser, and small ledger weights—known
as bell sinkers in North America.

Disgorger

Disgorger
A disgorger is essential if a fish swallows the hook.
Place the disgorger's groove on a taut line and run it into the fish's
mouth. It should be easy to gently nudge or turn the hook free.

Hooks

Hooks
You should always have a variety of sizes of barbless hooks.

Beads

If you're ledgering—for carp, say—you'll need a good quantity of pierced beads.

Floats

All-round anglers will have a selection of floats, from feature finder floats through to locslide floats for margin fishing. It's best to build up your collection slowly so you can find how each one behaves and how best to use it.

Pliers

Pliers allow you to position shot perfectly on a line. Long-handled pliers make a good disgorger.

Lures

Bear in mind when you're building up your collection that light conditions can vary so much within the course of a day's fishing that you often need different colored floats. Depending on what you're fishing for, you should have a variety of the most commonly used lures. Ask for advice from your local tackle shop. Fly-fishermen will have a wide selection of flies.

Forceps

Forceps are used for removing bigger hooks from specimen fish. If you fish for carp, in particular, you must also have an unhooking mat. You should never lay fish on hard ground.

Starlites

A low-cost way of illuminating a float at night, starlites are activated by breaking a seal and mixing two chemicals to create a luminous glow. This normally lasts for around four hours and is clearly visible within reasonable range of the bank.

Scales

You can choose between clock-face or spring-balance scales.

Swimfeeders

Keep a selection of open-ended swimfeeders in your tackle box.

Beads

Pole float

Finder

Fly lures

Lures

Forceps

Swimfeeders

TACKLE BOX ITEMS

Other Equipment

Apart from fundamentals like tackle, there's a whole range of equipment to make freshwater fishing a comfortable and pleasurable experience.

UMBRELLAS AND BIVOUACS

You'll often need protection from the elements, especially if you're intending to spend a fair amount of time at one spot. Depending on how comfortable you intend to be, you can buy anything from a standard umbrella to an extremely luxurious bivvie—which is what all anglers call bivouacs.

If you're river fishing and want to stay mobile, you can do without an umbrella if you've invested in good-quality protective clothing and waterproof gear. At the most sophisticated end of the market, you can buy double-skinned bivvies with built-in groundsheets that provide a great deal of comfort. You can accessorize bivvies like these with anything from mosquito nets to front tunnels for storing all kinds of equipment.

FOLDING/BEDCHAIRS

Always take a fully-sprung, low and comfortable chair with you when you're planning a long session. The key thing with a low chair is to make sure that it has wide, anti-sink feet to stop it descending into soft mud.

A bedchair is necessary for overnight sessions. The best bedchairs are almost completely flat and have three sets of adjustable legs for good stability. Look for a bedchair that has a firm locking position so that you can put the head rest in the position you want.

SEAT BOXES

Seat boxes are often more convenient than a folding chair because they cut down the amount of gear you carry. They're often higher, which may be more comfortable.

CLOTHING

You'll need light, comfortable, breathable and one hundred percent waterproof clothing, depending on the time of year and conditions you're fishing in. Whatever you buy, make sure outer garments are at least one size too big so you can wear thermal clothing underneath.

In winter, pay particular attention to keeping your head, hands, and feet warm. You should always wear a decent hat—this goes for summer too, when you need protection from the sun. Neoprene gloves, fingerless or otherwise, are good.

Moon boots or thigh waders are excellent for your feet in winter. Any landing or keepnets you buy should be made of the softest possible material to make sure you avoid damaging fish.

NETS

When you're fishing for smaller species, especially on rivers, you'll need spoon-shaped landing nets. These are less likely to get tangled in vegetation. It's always worth using a telescopic handle with this kind of net.

WEIGHT SLINGS

Specialist anglers keep fish they want to photograph in a carp sack. The most useful of these are the lightweight, compact combination sack/weight slings which you can easily fit into small spaces.

UNHOOKING MATS

Always use an unhooking mat when banks are hard and bumpy.

OTHER EQUIPMENT

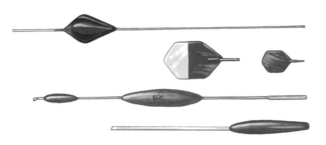

Typical types of float include:

◀ Pole floats.

◀ Feature finders.

◀ Surface controllers.

◀ Locslide floats.

Float Fishing

Any serious angler will admit that having a float to watch is one of the fundamental pleasures of fishing. It just isn't the same without a float.

There are an enormous number of floats to choose from. This means that the only way you can find out which is the best for specific conditions is through a process of trial and error.

Whichever float you decide you're most comfortable with, there are two things to bear in mind: visibility and weight.

Your float shouldn't be too light. It's far better if they're heavier and weighted sensitively. Whatever you're doing, the key thing is to make sure that the float is always clearly visible—light conditions vary constantly.

In certain parts of North America, float fishing also refers to a method of fishing from a boat. You launch your boat at one point of access on a particular stream or river and fish while floating downstream to the designated take-out point. This is particularly popular in Alabama. There are a number of methods of float fishing that have evolved over time, particularly in the UK. The following are just a few of them.

TROTTING

Trotting is simply running a float down the current in a number of different situations:

- When you're fishing a long, uniform, gravelly stretch of river.
- Under high banks with overhanging foliage.
- Along the junction of two flows that form a crease.

In high water, trotting under steep, vertical banks is a good way to fish the species that pack into these undercuts. For trotting, you should ideally use a fourteen foot rod, stick floats, and a floating line coated with silicon spray. Loose feed steadily with groundbait. Make sure that your float just clears the most shallow part of the swim.

STRET PEGGING

This is laying a float on the streamy water bordering a crease, where you can sometimes catch bigger specimens of fish. You'll use the same tackle as when float fishing with a rod-rest. As you are fishing on a tight line, you may get savage bites. It's important to keep your hand on the rod-butt in case it flips into the river. Dusk is a good time for stret pegging.

LAYING ON

Laying on is similar to stret pegging but done in still waters or very sluggish flows. A typical time for laying on is while fishing in overgrown still waters at dawn. Use a waggler float, fished bottom end only with the line sunk between the float and top rod.

THE LIFT METHOD

A very precise technique excellent for still water float fishing, the principle is similar to laying on. The difference is that the bottom shot is usually fished much closer to the hook. Lift-float fishing at night for carp using an inert waggler fitted with a night light can be thrilling.

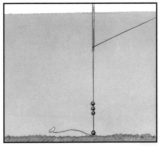

Open-ended swimfeeder

Closed-end swimfeeder

USING A SWIMFEEDER

Swimfeeders are used to deposit feed in the same spot you are fishing. There are two sorts: open-ended swimfeeders and closed-end feeders. Open-ended swimfeeders are used with groundbait that stays in the swimfeeder until it hits the water. The groundbait loosens and falls towards the bottom. Closed-end feeders use bait, like maggots, that leaves the swimfeeder when it hits the bottom.

There are no hard and fast rules but maggots packed in groundbait can be used in open-ended feeders. Commercial catfish baits and loose groundbait can be used in closed-end swimfeeders.

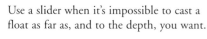

SLIDER FLOAT FISHING

Use a slider when it's impossible to cast a float as far as, and to the depth, you want.

You can convert any float into a slider by making it free-running on the line, stopping at the right depth with a sliding top knot and bead. The slider is easily adjusted to the depth you're fishing at by moving the knot and bead.

DRIFT FLOATS

A drift float is designed to catch the wind and be easily visible at long range. Drift float fishing allows you to search water at all ranges and any depths. To work well, your line needs to be continually greased and the wind behind you.

WAGGLER FLOATS

A waggler is any float attached at the bottom only. Fishing with a waggler is very common in still waters.

Ledgering

Ledgering is the British name for a number of different approaches to bottom fishing, which use sensitive bite indicators and terminal tackle that suits each one.

You're far more likely to catch fish such as carp or catfish ledgering than if you fish in the traditional American way, with a large hook and several ounces of weight. Fishing this way means you miss the fish more often than you catch them.

If you're going to try ledgering, you can adopt one of two different terminal tackle schemes: the paternoster rig or the link ledger.

THE PATERNOSTER

This is a rig which was originally developed for ocean fishing and then adapted for freshwater.

You tie a bell sinker onto the end of the line and place a loop four to twelve inches from the weight. Then you attach a leader and hook to the loop. You can also use a swivel instead of a loop and there are ways of making a loop without using a knot.

Remember that the loop-to-weight distance, which is called the link, must always be shorter than the leader. The baited hook will float down while your line is tight against the sinker.

In still water, you can use a leader of up to six feet but the link must never be longer that twenty-four inches. When you cast, the weight heads for the bottom, trailing the hook. Just before the rig hits the bottom, or when it does, you start reeling in to move the sinker toward you and tighten the line.

This straightens the leader and gives an appealing action to the bait, which fish often go for. With the paternoster, strikes will be rapid because fish tend to feel the weight of the sinker pretty quickly.

Some species will also reject the bait once they feel lead, which is why you must pay attention to the indicator when you use the rig.

In moving water, you can use a shorter leader and link. As the leader is always longer, your links will be between four and eight inches and the leader between twelve and twenty-four inches. The motion of the water will straighten the leader so you'll need to achieve a tight line by reeling it in.

REMEMBER

When fish are tentative biters, use a short leader and shorter link.

LEDGER LINK RIGS

Fishing with a static ledger link is the most popular bottom fish method in North America. You use a sinker crimped onto the line with four to eighteen inches of line left before the hook is tied on.

As far as weights are concerned, you can use a bell sinker, large split shot, or swimfeeders. Each of these is used for specific purposes, with or without a link.

In Europe, there are a number of sophisticated booms and other methods of creating a running ledger but they're not widely available in the United States.

To create a simple running ledger, place a bell sinker directly on the line and use a small split shot to keep it from running onto the hook. Connect the hook to a leader with breaking strength that is less than the main line, attached loop to loop to a swivel.

Since this is a good strategy for long range casting, many carp anglers use it widely.

REMEMBER

You can also use a heavy shot clipped to both sides of a length of line looped over the main line. Called the swan shot ledger, this is good for moving water where the bottom is rocky or snag-filled.

HOOKS

Bottom feeders can often be big fish so they can hook themselves with a lot of force, which is why you need a decent-sized hook.

Try using a short-to-medium shanked forged hook, tied to the leader with a strong knot. You need to check the link and knot regularly because this part of the set-up will take a beating between catching fish and setting up the rig after you cast. Replace the leader as often as you need to.

RODS AND REELS

The most common set-up for bottom fishing is a spincast rod and reel combination propped up on a forked stick, or in a single rod holder. You wait for a clear indication of a strike, which is most likely to be the fish pulling the rod into the water, before you set the hook.

As you can wait a long time for a good strike, it's important to check the hook to make sure your bait hasn't been stolen.

Some anglers add bells or other indicators to the line or rod tip to alert them to a bite.

You can use almost any good spinning reel with a ledger rod. Look for reels which can be set on free spool or have quickly adjustable drags, particularly if you're using the same reels for both carp and catfish.

Really, though, you should experiment until you find a reel with which you feel comfortable.

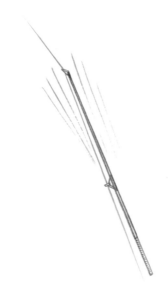

QUIVERTIPPING

Quivertips are more refined rod tip indicators that consist of a thin fiberglass tip spliced into the rod or screwed in by a special rod tip. You can use quivertips in a variety of sizes, lengths, or resistances, according to the conditions.

Cast a heavy weight—$3/4$ oz or more—and reel in the line until the tip arcs slightly. If you strike a fish the weight will make the tip move. It will soon become easy for you to read the quivertip and know when to strike.

You can use the quivertip in fast-moving water with excellent results.

SWINGTIPPING

Swingtips were invented in the 1950s to catch shy biting bream. Today, you can find swingtips of different sizes and weights for different conditions. Swingtips are particularly good for still or slowly moving rivers or streams and allow you to see just about every bite.

The most common swingtip setup is a paternoster terminal rig, three rod rests and a seat close to the handle of the rod.

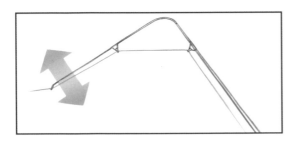

BANK STICKS

Unfortunately, it's very difficult to find a good rod rest in North America but the bank stick is an important part of ledgering systems. The position of the rod is crucial to your success. The best rod rests come in a number of different lengths and are made from aluminum or stainless steel.

Cheap rod rests will wear out quickly and are not very stable. If you are serious about fishing—particularly if you are, or intend to be, a specimen angler—it's worth investing in a set of British bank sticks.

PREPARING THE WATER

In Europe, anglers always ledger over baited areas. It's often far more difficult to attract fish than it is in North American waters, where it's easier to pinpoint where they will be.

Good use of feeding—or chumming as it is also known—can make a real difference to your fishing.

Chumming is an integral part of ledgering but it can take time before it shows results. However, if you start to add free offerings to your favorite fishing spot

you can greatly increase your chances of catching fish.

For instance, if you feed the same bait again and again at the same place, you'll find that fish will alter their behavior and look for where you're feeding, assuming you pick a spot which has an obvious structure. Serious carp anglers may well pick a gravel bar and feed it for an entire season to attract a single fish.

Try using a slingshot and put several ounces of sweetcorn at the head of a pool where the fish you want to catch are. Or try using maggots. If you don't feed too much or too often, the fish will find your bait quickly.

A word of warning; chumming is illegal in some states so check before you chum.

TOUCH LEDGERING

This is keeping the line in your hand when you're waiting for a strike. You need no rod rests and you can feel a strike easily because you're in direct contact with the fish. This method requires constant attention and is so sensitive that you might find that you strike too early. Touch ledgering is a method for experts.

Game Fishing

Going after game fish, cunning hunters themselves, is an especially exciting challenge. You can use a variety of techniques and baits depending on the fish you're looking for.

LIVEBAITING

Many game fish, like Northern pike or muskie, will be attracted by live fish of the species that they naturally eat such as sculpin or minnow. If you're ledgering using livebait, it needs to be lightly paternostered and used near a suitable predator fish ambush point, for example, heavy vegetation.

Whenever you're livebaiting, it's important to use a float that's big enough. If not, the bait will pull the float under and keep it there. If the float disappears out of sight you won't know if you've got a bite.

DEADBAITING

Deadbaiting is becoming particularly popular as more and more anglers decide that livebaiting is unacceptable. It can be used for any predatory game fish and the most common baits are minnows, herrings, and mackerel. Whole sardines are especially good for large fish but they need to be frozen.

This is why a good cool box is an essential purchase if you're serious about going after game fish.

Minnow is one of the most common freshwater deadbaits, particularly when you're fishing for crappie. When you're fishing for salmon, try fresh, frozen, or cured anchovies.

Some anglers add extra flavor to deadbaits by using fish oils such as mackerel. Flavoring deadbait can make a real difference when you're fishing on large areas of windswept still water, where currents below the surface will waft the trails around. You can also make deadbait more attractive by coloring them.

Paternoster Livebait

Deadbait Ledger

Marabou jigs

SMALL LURES

Small lures are particularly effective when you're fishing for crappie. You can try:

• *Marabou jigs:* these are small jigs that have furry bodies, puffy, feathery tails, and come in a wide variety of sizes and colors.

• *Curly-tail grubs:* these are soft plastic baits that have curly tails on the back and produce lots of action when you jig or retrieve them steadily.

LURES

Artificial lures will simulate anything eaten by fish. They can be made of balsa wood, plastic, metal, or rubber and can contain anything from a single to three hooks. You can use artificial lures on the bottom, middle depths, or surface.

Any game fish can be caught using a lure. Lures imitate the prey of predatory fish, not necessarily in appearance but more in behavior. Most game fish react strongly to sudden movement and vibration and it's these factors that are mimicked by lures.

A good thing about lure fishing is the fact that you don't need much additional equipment. If you do become keen on the technique, a bait-casting rod of around nine foot is ideal. You also need a good, strong reel that ideally is vibration-free and has a reliable, fighting, drag system.

Thin, supple trace wire—no less than 15 lbs is vital but this should be stronger when you're fishing for aggressive, larger fish.

SPINNERS

A spinner is a lure with a rotating blade to create vibration. They are particularly versatile and you can use them to catch bass, bluegill, catfish, pike, and crappie. Listed below is a selection of spinners commonly used when fishing for crappie:

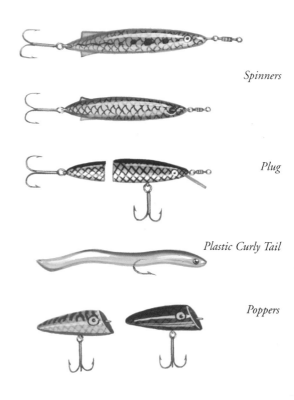

Spinners

Plug

Plastic Curly Tail

Poppers

- *Small willow leaf blade:* a very effective type of blade that works well when rigged with a two inch tube bait or curly tail.

- *Small silver colorado (circular) blade:* this is excellent in stained, dark water because it produces a lot of vibrations and can be fished very slowly.

- *Small gold blade:* this is a tiny, gold Colorado blade with a $1/32$ oz jig head and a two-inch tube bait that works well with just about any freshwater species.

- *Beetle spin:* these come in all kinds of colors and sizes but try the $1/8$ and $1/16$ oz varieties.

Spoon

A spoon is a flat piece of metal shaped like a spoon which wobbles, when retrieved. The key to effective use of spinners and spoons with any fish is how quickly and how much you vary your retrieve after you've cast. Your retrieval should always be calm, slow, and controlled and you should occasionally flip the lure over to one side to create additional vibration.

GENERAL GUIDELINES

Clear stained

Vibration-brightness

Cloudy

Bright   *Night*

When it comes to knowing the color of lure to choose, the only way you can establish which will be the most effective is by trial and error. In clear, and lightly stained, water you need to match the natural food items—use natural-looking colors like smoke, gray or silver when using a minnow type lure. Vibration and brightness are key to attracting strikes in dark or muddy water—try fishing at midday or in bright sunlight using brightly colored spinners, grubs, and jigs.

Cloudy, overcast days limit the amount of sunlight that reaches the fish so try using browns, greens, or even black. On bright, sunny days simply choose the brightest color that you have. If you're fishing at night, the best things to try are jet-black lures or combinations of black and another color.

Fly-fishing

Fly-fishing is probably the most sporting and difficult angling method but is also the one with the most dedicated following. It is widely used for catching trout in North America but it can also be effective with other fish, including bluegill, bonefish, and carp.

One of the reasons anglers are so passionate about fly-fishing is because it's a vast subject and mastering the techniques takes years. You can start by getting the basics right.

When fly-fishing, anglers start with basic equipment that includes:

- a rod of between seven and twelve feet long,
- lines that have been coated with various different kinds of plastics so that they can float or sink rapidly or slowly,
- a nylon leader added to the end of the line once the fly line has been wound on to the ring spool—fly leaders are a lot lighter than the actual fly line to let an angler cast easily,
- fly lure—these are intended to imitate an insect that the fish feed on. They can be made of feathers, hairs, or synthetic materials tied to a single hook and usually have no weight.

FLY LURES

Fly lures come in a variety of shapes, colors, and sizes with many dedicated anglers making their own. They may be designed to look like aquatic insects in their nymphal, pupal, or adult state and may be as large as a golf ball. To give one example, trout anglers often use nymphs—when fishing in lakes they may use flies that look like the nymphs of dragonflies or damselflies. These are weighted and fished on, or near, the bottom.

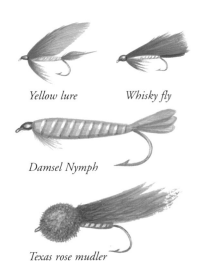

Yellow lure   *Whisky fly*

Damsel Nymph

Texas rose mudler

REMEMBER

The type of lure to use depends on the time of year that you're fishing.

FLY-FISHING

STARTING OUT

Starting out in fly-fishing means gathering together a decent tackle system and understanding how to assemble it. Without any assistance, this is easier said than done. Most novices start by getting advice at the store where they bought their equipment. You can also try friends who fly-fish or one of the many fly-fishing clubs all across America.

If you're determined to go it alone, this simple guide to preparing, using, and storing your tackle should be helpful.

THE TACKLE COMPONENTS

For fly-fishing you will need:
- a rod
- a reel
- backing
- a fly line
- a leader or tippet material
- flies

Systems very rarely come totally assembled and ready to use. You need to attach the various components before you are ready to use the tackle.

Fly line

Fly line-tapering/ sinking-double tape, comes in various different colours.

Braided Backing

Braided backing is put directly onto the reel. The fly line is attached to this followed by the tippet or leader to the fly.

Leader or tippet

REMEMBER

All fly rods are weight numbered so lines have to be the right weight for the rod ie. 5-6-7-8-9

Backing onto reel   *Fly line onto reel*   *Leader or tippet*   *Fly*

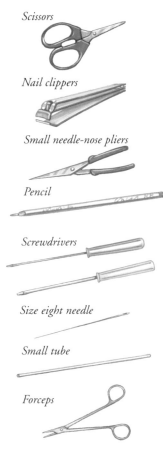

Scissors

Nail clippers

Small needle-nose pliers

Pencil

Screwdrivers

Size eight needle

Small tube

Forceps

Before you start to assemble your tackle, find a well-lit area with a chair and a table. You'll need to have to hand:

- a pair of small scissors,
- nail clippers,
- small needle-nose pliers,
- a pencil,
- some small screwdrivers,
- a size eight needle,
- a small strawlike tube or large needle,
- flexible nail polish or fly head cement.

SETTING UP THE REEL

First of all, you need to decide which hand you'll use to reel in the line. It's best to use one hand to cast and fight the fish and the free hand to operate the reel. This will be the left hand for right-handed casters and vice versa. Most reels are set up to retrieve with the right hand. If it can be converted, there should be instructions with the reel and you can use a small screwdriver for the conversion. Once the reel is set up, attach it to the reel seat on the rod's butt section. The reel should be hanging below the rod and the reel handle should be on the correct side for the hand you've decided to use to crank the reel. Its line guard should be facing forward.

FLY ROD

Your fly rod and reel should always be carried in protective cases. If they weren't supplied, it's important to purchase ones made out of aluminum or fiberglass. It sounds obvious, but when you buy separate cases make sure they fit your equipment.

ASSEMBLING THE FLY ROD

Most rods are two-piece and you connect them with a single ferrule connection. Never push, force, or twist the ferrule in case you damage the rod. Look down the rod to make sure the sections are in a straight line.

To avoid damaging your rod, don't ever lay it down or prop it against an irregular surface. Be careful around doors or car trunks in particular.

ATTACHING THE FLY REEL

Most fly reels will be damaged if you drop them onto a hard surface. When you're positioning the reel, make sure the handle is on the proper side and tighten it, but without using excess pressure.

LINE PULLING

To pull line through the rod's guides, start by finding the leader's end and pull out ten to fifteen feet of fly line from the reel. Use one hand to hold the rod and the other to pull line. Don't lay the rod down and pull the line out, as you will get grit in the reel and cause damage. Double the fly line over about two feet from the leader and pass the doubled end through each guide, pulling the line and leader after it. To straighten the leader and fly line, hold the fly line just above the junction knot. Hold the leader at the junction with both hands and begin pulling, using sliding strokes, down toward the leader tip. Heating, stretching, and cooling will straighten the leader.

Attaching the fly reel

DRESSING THE FLY LINE

If you're using a floating fly line and want to clean or dress it with waterproof floatant, do it while the fly line is stretched, using a clean cloth or dressing applicator.

Fly lines that are regularly cleaned and dressed will always last longer and perform better.

ATTACHING THE FLY

The most practical and versatile knot is the Duncan loop. This loop is adjustable so the fly can be held tightly or loosely. If you want to hold or store the fly temporarily before you begin casting it, or between fishing sessions, put the fly in the rod's hook-keeper and tighten it so it doesn't fall out.

LOOKING AFTER YOUR TACKLE

Forgetting about your tackle after a day's fishing and neglecting it, or taking it apart or storing it incorrectly, are easily done.

Following the straightforward steps below will help you avoid problems.

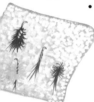

- Remove the fly by cutting it off the leader and carefully storing it in an open area like your hat band or vest fly-drying patch.

- Carefully, and evenly, wind your fly line and leader back onto the reel, cleaning and drying it with a towel—don't wind the line onto the reel too tightly or loosely.

- After you've removed the reel from the rod, wipe it clean with a towel and put it in its storage bag or case, but leave this open so any moisture can evaporate.

- Take your fly rod apart by taking a firm grip on the two sections and pulling the ferrules apart, being careful not to bend or twist either section.

- Use a towel or cloth to dry and clean the rod; remove dirt or greasy film using a spray window-cleaner.

STORAGE

If you look after your equipment properly, it's always a pleasure to use and less likely to fail when you've hooked a great fish. You should always keep your rod and reel in a cool, dry, and dark place away from sunlight. Try not to seal either the rod or reel case if they're going to be stored for a long time.

If you do have to store them for a few months, it makes sense to remove the line from the reel, clean it and store it in large, loose coils to make it last longer. Fly lines have soft, flexible coatings or finishes that will deform if left tight on a reel for a long time.

Fly fishing for carp

Fly-fishermen, fishing in warm waters, often accidentally catch carp. Deliberately fly-fishing for carp provides an interesting variation on traditional carp-fishing techniques.

There are two ways to fly-fish for carp. Sight casting involves looking for carp in the water and casting your fly one or two feet in front of them. If carp are tailing in the shallows it's because they're eating the organisms they find on the bottom. When they take your fly, expect exciting fishing.

FLY-FISHING

With blind casting, you cast to places where carp are likely to be and hope you're right. A better way is to use chum to concentrate fish in a particular area.

Probably the single most effective way to fish for carp with a fly is to choose a fly that sinks to the bottom, hook point up, and stirs the mud or silt when you twitch it.

Carp feed by cruising along the bottom vacuuming up whatever they find but they are also usually watching for prey that might leave puffs on the bottom. These might be crayfish, a leech, or a mayfly nymph.

Janet Fischer with a Carp

REMEMBER

Please remember that chumming is not legal in certain states.

CARP FLIES

As with all fly-fishing, the best way to catch carp is by using a fly that imitates food they recognize:

- *Aquatic creatures:* the larval and pupal stages of aquatic insects like mayflies, dragonflies, and damselflies, small aquatic organisms like leeches, worms, scuds, immature crayfish, and small baitfish like sculpins.

larvie

- *Plant material:* including the fluffy seeds of the cottonwood tree and mulberries.

- *Introduced food:* foods that we put into the water that carp learn to eat, like sweetcorn, dog food, and bread.

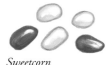

Sweetcorn

There are flies that imitate all of these items. Carp are extremely sensitive to taste and smell, so remember to rub your fly with mud or algae from the bank or bottom of the river or lake. Although the mud comes off with the first cast, it will leave a natural taste and smell on your fly. This will mask your own odor.

Distressed damsel

Walkers mayfly

Bloodworm

Czech Nymph

Wooly worm

Cased Caddis

Artificial floaters

Bread   Corn

Try the following flies pictured and discussed here.

- *Dragonfly nymph:* if you're lake fishing.

- *All round hex nymph:* if you're using this in a river, cast above where the carp are and let it drift down to them.

- *Generic and rollover scud:* these flies mimic the behavior of the small, freshwater, shrimp-like creatures.

- *Bristle leech:* which sits on the bottom and creates a puff of silt when you retrieve it.

- *Rollover worm:* where the hook rides up as the fly sinks but flips over when you retrieve the fly.

- *Carp booby:* these are floating flies which imitate baitfish and are made to hover near the bottom.

- *Corn fly:* an artificial hair rig sponge fly.

- *Purple mulberry fly:* for fishing in waters which have overhanging mulberry trees.

Responsible Fishing

If you're going to take fishing seriously, there's a code of practice followed by all responsible anglers.

CATCH AND RELEASE

When it comes to careful handling of fish that you intend to release, there are a number of basic dos and don'ts:

- Always handle fish with wet hands—dry hands will damage a fish's protective coating.
- Return the fish to the water immediately if possible.
- Use barbless hooks.
- Always use a disgorger of some sort to remove hooks.
- Don't lift fish out of the water using your line but use a landing net.
- Fish over ten pounds should be weighed using a weigh bag.

USING A KEEP NET

Careful anglers who want to retain a catch to photograph and weigh later, follow a set of rules to make sure the fish is treated as cautiously as possible:

- Under no circumstances should you keep more than one fish in a keep sack.

- If you're pegging the sack out in water, make sure the material doesn't affect the fish's gills.
- In hot water, where there's only shallow water in the margins, you need to ask yourself whether it's right to use the keep net at all.

With big fish, kept in running water, aim for a steady flow of water through the sack and always make certain the head is facing upstream.

If at all possible, you should try to peg out a rigid structure that allows the fish to breathe normally and recover fast. These structures follow the Queenford retention system and are used for anything from the smallest perch to the largest catfish.

RESPONSIBLE FISHING

Large fish that are known for fighting themselves to a standstill should always be retained for some time after they've been caught. This way they can recover in safety. It's every angler's responsibility to handle and return fish to the water as carefully as possible.

RESPECTING OTHER ANGLERS

When you're fishing, always respect another angler's space. If they're doing well, it's a major breach of etiquette to sit near them.

LOOKING AFTER THE ENVIRONMENT

You don't really become an angler unless you enjoy being close to nature. This is why most anglers have a well-deserved reputation for helping to maintain, not just clean, unpolluted waters but the whole of the surrounding environment.

RESPONSIBLE FISHING

There are a number of fundamental things to remember, which are mostly common sense.

- Don't drop litter or leave tackle discarded—nylon line is particularly dangerous to wildlife.
- Always clear away litter before you leave even if it isn't yours.
- Remove rigs that have been caught up in vegetation or underwater snags wherever you can.
- Report lost terminal tackle to water managers if you can't retrieve it.
- When you're choosing your swim, take extra care if you're in a place where people usually feed waterfowl—their expectations could lead to greater risk of entanglement.
- Never leave your rods unattended or with hooks still baited.
- Use a hook length of lower breaking strain than the reel line wherever possible.
- If you're using a bolt rig or fixed lead, make sure that if the line breaks it won't result in a fish or bird dragging a ledger around.
- Use barbless or reduced hooks wherever possible.
- Don't use lead weights: there are plenty of non-toxic weights available.
- Beware of birds swimming into your line or picking up surface baits.
- Take great care when you're fishing surface baits like bread or floaters as these may attract waterfowl.

RESPONSIBLE FISHING

REMOVING A HOOK

Sooner or later, most anglers will get a hook stuck in their flesh. The least painful way of removing a hook is to press down on the shank and reduce the grip of the barb. When you're pressing hardest, jerk the hook straight back in line with the shank quickly and powerfully.

Using this technique, the barb should slide cleanly out with very little, if any, flesh tearing.

SAFETY

The use of common sense should avoid most major incidents but the following are points to consider to ensure safe fishing.

• The most frequent accidents occur while wading. When you're wading, always make sure of the depth of the water between you and the bank by using a wading stick.

• Be very careful around overhead power lines and warn other anglers of the danger.

• Adhere to state limits for certain fishing.

• Most states will have set limits for the number and size of certain fish that you are allowed to catch.

• It's important to stick to these limits as there are many endangered species of fish in North America.

REMEMBER

Irresponsible fishing means that all anglers suffer.

Fish Recipes

Nearly all of the freshwater fish that you can catch in North America make excellent eating. Here are a few simple recipes.

Ingredients

½ lb smallmouth bass, filleted

5 tablespoons butter

Salt and pepper

⅓ cup of yellow cornmeal

⅓ cup flour

1 tablespoon vinegar

Parsley to garnish

Sautéed Smallmouth Bass

Dredge the fillets in a mix of cornmeal, flour, salt, and pepper. Sautée slowly in melted butter over a medium heat until well browned. Turn over and brown the other side.

When the fish has turned opaque, remove to a warm platter and garnish with parsley. Add the vinegar to the juices in the pan, heat and pour over the fish.

Fried Potato and Walleye Fillets

Mix the eggs, milk, and parsley flakes in a bowl and season to taste. Pour the instant potato flakes into a separate bowl. Dip the walleye fillets into the egg/milk mixture and then into the potato flakes. Fry in a hot pan with the melted lard and butter until brown.

Ingredients

- 4 medium size walleye fillets cut in pieces
- 2 cups instant potato flakes
- 2 eggs
- 1 cup milk
- 2 tablespoons parsley flakes
- $1/3$ cup lard
- $1/3$ cup butter
- Seasoning to taste

Crispy Crappie

Take twenty-five large crappie fillets and cut into one-inch pieces, place in a bowl of ice water and refrigerate for fifteen minutes. Mix the tempura fish batter according to the packet instructions. Then add the garlic powder, salt and ground black pepper, and a little ice-cold water and mix. Add the soy sauce and lemon juice.

Remove the cut fish from ice water and dab with a paper towel to remove any excess water. Dip in batter and deep fry, or shallow fry in enough hot oil to cover the fish pieces completely.

Ingredients

- 25 crappie fillets
- Store-bought tempura fish batter
- $1/2$ teaspoon garlic powder
- Salt and ground pepper
- $1/2$ teaspoon soy sauce
- 2 tablespoons lemon juice
- Chilled water

Ingredients

2 lbs Northern pike fillet,
cut in 2-inch cubes

1 sweet bell pepper

1 medium onion, chopped

$^1/_2$ can carrots, julienned

$^1/_2$ cup celery, chopped

$^1/_4$ cup olive oil

2 tablespoons lemon juice

4 oz vegetable broth

4 oz coconut milk

3 teaspoons curry powder

1 teaspoon turmeric

4 cups rice

Salt and pepper to taste

Curried Northern Pike

Prepare rice according to the package directions. Lightly coat the fish in several tablespoons of olive oil. Sprinkle with the turmeric and salt, if desired. Place in a baking dish, sprinkle with the lemon juice. Bake at 400°F until the fish starts to flake slightly.

While the fish is in the oven, briefly sauté the vegetables in the remaining oil. Add the broth, and curry powder, reduce the heat to a simmer. Add the fish, rinse the baking dish with the coconut milk to deglaze the dish.

Add the coconut milk to the fish and vegetable mixture and simmer until the fish starts to flake. Place on a serving dish and serve with rice, fresh fruit, and flat bread on the side.

Ingredients

Bluegill fillets

1 can of potato soup

Pint of milk

Fresh, minced onion

1 teaspoon parsley

Bluegill Chowder

Dilute the can of potato soup with milk, heat until simmering. Add fresh, minced onion to taste and a level teaspoon of parsley. Simmer until the onions are transparent. Add salt and pepper to taste. Add the bluegill fillets and stew until they're translucent.

Seared Salmon

Heat a large frying pan over a medium heat. Add the butter. When melted, add the garlic, teriyaki sauce, and vermouth, stirring to blend the flavors. Dredge salmon fillets in flour, add to pan and cover. Cook for five minutes each side.

Remove from heat, letting the salmon sit in the covered pan for another five minutes. Garnish with parsley and/or green onions. Serve with wild rice.

Ingredients

- 2-4 lbs skinned salmon fillets
- 6 teaspoons butter
- 1 cup flour
- 6 teaspoons teriyaki sauce
- 4 teaspoons dry vermouth
- 4 chopped cloves of garlic
- Parsley and green onions to garnish

Barbecued Bullhead

For the sauce place all the ingredients, apart from the fish, in a saucepan. Heat until the honey begins to bubble. Stir well and remove from the heat. Set aside.

Dot the bullhead fillets with butter and place on a piece of aluminum on a barbecue grill about twelve inches from the hot coals. Cook the fillets for about four minutes covered and baste with the barbecue sauce. Cook for another two minutes until the fish is done and flakes.

Remove fish to a serving platter and serve with the remaining sauce on the side. This is excellent served with steamed rice and green vegetables.

Ingredients

- 8 bullhead fillets
- 4 oz honey
- 2 tablespoons soy sauce
- Juice from one lemon
- 1/4 cup sherry
- 2 tablespoons olive oil
- 1 teaspoon rosemary
- 1/2 teaspoon dried ginger
- 1/2 teaspoon dried thyme
- 2 tablespoons butter

With the proliferation of
state records for different
fish, it's sometimes
difficult to keep up to
date with current
freshwater fish records.
If keeping a track of
record fish is part of your
enjoyment of the sport,
you'll need to read the
specialist magazines
and visit dedicated
websites regularly.

Vital Statistics

Here are some vital statistics for most of the fish featured in this guide.

Fish	World record weight
Sea-run Atlantic salmon	79 lbs 2 oz
Landlocked Atlantic salmon	22 lbs 11 oz
Bighead carp	75 lbs 8 oz
Brook trout	14 lbs 8 oz
Brown bullhead	11 lbs
Chinook salmon	97 lbs 4 oz
Flathead catfish	123 lbs
Lake trout	66 lbs 8 oz
Lake whitefish	14 lbs 6 oz
Largemouth bass	22 lbs 4 oz
Muskie	69 lbs 15 oz
Northern pike	55 lbs
Rainbow trout	31 lbs 6 oz
Smallmouth bass	11 lbs 15 oz
Steelhead	42 lbs
Yellow perch	4 lbs 3oz
Walleye	25 lbs
White crappie	5 lbs 3 oz
White sturgeon	1387 lbs

FISHING ASSOCIATIONS

You may want to know more about your chosen quarry. Perhaps you want to meet fellow anglers who share your fascination with one specific species. Maybe you're going on a fishing vacation, and want to know more about where to go or the area you've chosen. Either way here are some associations and clubs for a few of the fish featured in this book.

American Crappie Association
PO Box 848,
Brentwood
TN
37024-0848
Tel: (615) 377 7800

South East Michigan Bass Association (SEMBA)
PO Box 1017, Monroe
MI
48161

Missouri Muskies
PO Box 5, Hermitage
MO
65668

Carp Anglers Group
PO Box 1502, Bartlesville
OK
74005-1502
Tel: (918) 335 3062

Fish Hawks
PO Box 700, Forked River
NJ
08731

Boca Raton Fishing Club
951 NW 13th Street, Suite 2-E
Boca Raton, Florida
33486
Tel: (561) 995 1929

Pacific Salmon Foundation
Vancouver, British Columbia
V6J 4S6
Tel: (604) 664 7664

Truchas Chapter Trout Unlimited
PO Box 31671, Santa Fe
NM
87594-1671

North East Bass Association
Maine, Massachusetts, Connecticut, Virginia

Conclusion

As said at the beginning of this book, it's a handy source of reference. If you're already a keen angler, you'll know that learning about your favorite quarry and how to catch it can take years.

There's no substitute for going out and actually trying to catch the fish, but there is a wealth of specialist magazines, books, videos, and web sites dedicated to particular species. Keeping up to date with the information that is available is a vital part of serious angling.

Even if you're the most dedicated specimen carp angler, you'll hopefully have been pleasantly surprised to learn something new from this book. We hope it will spur you on to try some of the suggested techniques on your favorite fish—going fly-fishing for carp, for instance. Maybe it has triggered a desire to try something different.

Who knows, you may have already booked your ticket to go fishing for the mighty Australian Murray cod.

However you've been inspired by this book, good luck with your fishing.

So, as they say, tight lines!